GOD'S LAW OF ATTRACTION: The Believer's Guide to Success and Fulfillment

SUSAN LEE

The information in this book is based on personal experience and
opinion and is intended for general reference and should not be
substituted for personal verification by users. The author and
publisher disclaim any personal liability for the advice presented on
these pages. All effort has been made to verify the accuracy of the
information, but we assume no responsibility for errors, inaccuracies
or omissions.

c/o R50 Books
PO Box 441024
Aurora, CO 80044
www.R50Books.com
crew@R50Books.com

CONTENTS

FREE BONUS

1	INTRODUCTION	1
2	LAW OF ATTRACTION THROUGH THE YEARS	7
3	WHAT IS THE LAW OF ATTRACTION REALLY?	11
4	PUTTING GOD'S LAW OF ATTRACTION TO WORK	21
5	STEP ONE: ASK	25
6	STEP TWO: BELIEVE	33
7	STEP THREE: ACT	41
8	STEP FOUR: ALLOW	47
9	STEP FIVE: RECEIVE	57
10	OVERCOMING COMMON CHALLENGES	61
11	FOLLOW THESE STEPS AND ACHIEVE GOD'S BEST!	69

FREE BONUS!

Thanks for purchasing God's Law of Attraction!

As a special gift for taking the time, I would like to provide you with access to **God's Law of Attraction Worksheets** which will help you determine your goals, create positive affirmations, and combat negative beliefs.

Also, you will receive two special collections, formatted for printing as reminder cards to be carried with you throughout the day:

Treasury of God's Promises is a collection of Bible verses that will help you focus on God's positive message.

Quotable Quotes is a selection of affirming quotes that will help you to keep God's powerful word in your heart.

In addition, you will be registered to receive new bonuses and gifts as they are added. To get all three gifts, just visit **R50Books.com/gloabonusreg**.

1
INTRODUCTION

*"If you need wisdom, ask our generous God, and He will give it to you.
He will not rebuke you for asking." (James 1:5)*

Several years ago, a friend of mine came home from a weekend seminar; full of praise for a movie that I just "had to see." I was intrigued since most of the time my friend isn't one to display strong emotion. Given that I'd not heard of this particular movie, I had no idea what to expect as I sat down to watch.

The movie was "The Secret;" a documentary based on the "Law of Attraction" (a term that I knew nothing about at the time). It began with a lot of creepy music and its producer, Rhonda Byrnes, telling a weird story about being at her "lowest point" before stumbling on the ancient "secret" that instantly made her rich and famous. Throughout the movie, my emotions ran the gamut: from amusement, motivation, and hope, to disdain, rejection, guilt and even fear.

My friend, who defines himself as an agnostic, saw the principles presented in "The Secret" as an amazing discovery that would immediately solve all his problems.

As a lifelong Christian, I was struggling to fit the message of the movie into the framework of my walk with God. While there was a LOT of silly mumbo jumbo in "The Secret" that was easy to dismiss, I also saw enough in the movie that aligned with my understanding of Christianity and the lessons I'd learned from the Bible to make me pretty confused when it was over.

Since "The Secret" came out, the Law of Attraction has been a big player in the self-help community. Its principles may be packaged in different ways depending upon the messenger, but it's the same idea nonetheless. As a Christian and self-improvement junkie, I began crossing paths with the Law of Attraction again and again, and the question of how this law fit in with my faith was one that I had to reconcile.

At this point, I *could* cue the mystical music and talk breathlessly about how I searched through ancient sources as one thing after another led me closer to "the truth" - but that's already been done - so I will just suffice to say that I kept my eyes and ears open over the years hoping to make some sense of the Law of Attraction and how I could apply its principles as a Christ follower.

I have concluded that Christians can apply the Law of Attraction in their own lives as it is a natural law *created* by God as a way to achieve the plans He has for us! Similar to the natural law of gravity, the Law of Attraction has been given by God to *everyone* to use - Christian or not - as an instrument of common grace. It may be packaged in different ways by different people, but the bottom line is God created it (as He created everything) and wants us to know and understand it in order to make our lives, and the lives of all His people, better.

Basically, the Law of Attraction states that everything that is presently in your life, both the good and the bad, is a result of your thoughts. If you are unhappy with your life (in debt, in a bad relationship, unhealthy, or *whatever*) you have only your own thoughts to blame. Another way to explain the Law of Attraction is that you will attract into your life more of whatever your focus, attention, and energy are upon.

Thus, according to the Law of Attraction, if you give a lot of attention to the negative things going on in your life, whatever they may be, you will reap more of the same. The good news (from the secular gurus) is that all you have to do is focus your thoughts on what you desire, believe you will receive it, and the "universe" will provide it to you.

The Bible backs up the basic principles of the Law of Attraction. Proverbs 23:7 tells us: *"For as he thinketh in his heart, so is he."* Unfortunately, the secular champions of the Law of Attraction often clothe the message in new-age, mystical, or downright creepy robes that send Christians running for cover. I mean, channeling spirit guides or declaring that WE can create EVERYTHING we desire, merely by thinking about it are just too far out there for Christians to embrace.

And, all the new age discussion over the "universe" manifesting our every desire seems to edge-out God in favor of the human EGO and makes Christians wonder if we can believe in or practice the Law of Attraction and still serve our God.

And yet, story after story in the Bible suggests there IS something to the Law of Attraction, and that by rejecting its validity outright, Christians today may be missing out on an important tool that God created to help us live out the life He intended and to fight the enemy of this world.

3

The Bleeding Woman

Take, for example, the story of the bleeding woman found in Mark 5: 25-35. It is about a woman who had been sick for twelve years. Maybe she had a fibroid tumor or some other chronic abnormality. Whatever caused it, this woman was suffering in a big way. Her constant bleeding had made her weak, exhausted, probably anemic, and humiliated and embarrassed as well. Bleeding was taboo in her culture, and so she was ceremonially unclean. That means she couldn't even *touch* another person while she was bleeding, which, remember, was *12 years*! Could you imagine never getting a hug or even a handshake from another person for twelve years?

She had tried every legitimate (and probably a good share of illegal) remedies and none was able to make her better, although many of the courses of treatment were undoubtedly terribly painful. She was tired, lonely, weak, out of money, forlorn, secluded and depressed. She really and truly was at the end of her rope.

Talk around the neighborhood was that a new guy in town, named Jesus, had been healing impossible cases: paralytics, diseased people and mentally ill. He had even cured two people that others had already declared dead! This woman knew, she absolutely *knew*, that this was the guy who could heal her once and for all.

The woman wanted to be cured with all her heart. She believed - truly believed - that Jesus could do it. She said, *"If I can just touch his clothes, that will be enough to heal me."* She touched him, breaking all social codes (remember, she was unclean). Immediately, she was cured! She asked for a cure, believed,

4

acted on that belief and received healing. The Law of Attraction defined.

2
LAW OF ATTRACTION THROUGH THE YEARS

"Faith is the substance of things hoped for, the evidence of things not seen." (Hebrews 11:1)

The principles of the Law of Attraction are by no means new, although the phrase "law of attraction" didn't exist until the early 1900s and the advent of the New Thought Movement. During the New Thought Movement, people began to promote the ideas that "infinite intelligence" is everywhere, sickness and lack originate in the mind, and "right thinking" has a healing effect. Popular authors from the New Thought Movement are Wallace Wattles, who wrote *The Science of Getting Rich* and William Atkinson, the author of *Thought Vibrations or the Law of Attraction in the Thought World.*

About 35 years after Wattles and Atkinson coined the phrase "Law of Attraction," Napoleon Hill promoted many of the principles introduced in their works in his blockbuster book *Think and Grow Rich*, including the belief that you attract the things you think about.

But long before the New Thought Movement, sometime

around 470 BC, in fact, there lived a Greek philosopher named Empedocles. Like many scholars of his time, he dedicated his life to studying how man relates to the universe as a whole. As was the norm at that time, he wrote his findings in the form of verse, with some of his works surviving to this day.

In much of Empedocles' work, he describes two forces - "love" and "strife". These are attractive and repulsive forces which penetrate the universe and work among people; while remaining unseen by the ordinary eye. They alternately hold empire over things, however, neither are ever quite absent. This theory by Empedocles is often considered the first written attempt to describe the Law of Attraction at work.

Around, 250 BC, Buddha simplified things in the *Dhammapada*, one of the most widely read and best known Buddhist scriptures, which said: *"We are what we think. All that we are arises with our thoughts. With our thoughts, we make the world."*

And the Biblical scripture, both the Old and New Testament, contains hundreds of references and stories that prescribe the principles of the Law of attraction. Matthew 7:7 tells us: *"Keep on asking, and you will receive what you ask for. Keep on seeking, and you will find. Keep on knocking, and the door will be opened to you."*

The 2006 film "The Secret" (and the book by the same name) by Rhonda Byrne, is based on the same principles of the Law of Attraction described by early philosophers and the authors from the New Thought Movement such as Wallace Wattles and Napoleon Hill. "The Secret," while packaged slightly differently, covers no new territory. However, it gained widespread acceptance due to attention from the likes of Oprah and Larry King; thus, more and more people are

8

actively applying the principles of the law of Attraction to their own lives.

3
WHAT IS THE LAW OF ATTRACTION – REALLY?

For the foolishness of God is wiser than human wisdom, and the weakness of God is stronger than human strength. (1 Corinthians 1:25)

The main question remains: what, really, is the Law of Attraction? Some people believe it is little more than warm and fuzzy self-help jargon - and about as helpful as a pat on the back and a positive *"you can do it!"* But what if there really is something more to it than positive cheerleading?

Others call it witchcraft, a "secret" ritual or spell you can learn that will magically bring you everything you ever wanted in life. But what if the Law of Attraction is much more natural and wholesome than witchcraft?

What if the Law of Attraction is really <u>God's</u> Law of Attraction?"

The principles of *"thought begets thought"* and *"for every action, there is a reaction"* have been present throughout both ancient

11

and modern history, which suggests that something happens when you apply the law. Common beliefs such as these *become* common because they work.

A question which must be answered is this: Because secular proponents of the Law of Attraction interpret and apply the law differently than we Christians do, does that make it any less real?

> *This is what the Lord says: "I would no more reject my people than I would change my laws that govern night and day, earth and sky."*
> *(Jeremiah 33:25)*

There are many natural laws that God has put in place to give us an orderly and predictable world in which to live. While non-believers may explain these natural laws differently; we as Christians know that God is the mastermind behind the miracle of chemistry, physics, planetary motion, the uniformity of nature and the law of logic, to name a few. We don't have to fully understand these natural laws to believe their reality. In this way, the Law of Attraction exists.

Just as we're confident that the elements in the periodic table will be comprised of the same chemical properties every time, we can be just as confident that the Law of Attraction will produce positive results in our lives. As Christians, we shouldn't fear the Law of Attraction any more than we fear chemistry. It is a gift from God.

The Differences

There are, however, decided differences as to how we, as Christians, will interpret and use the Law of Attraction as we strive to live our lives to the glory of God. Just as it would be wrong for us to apply our knowledge of chemistry to build a bomb that could hurt others, we should use the same level of diligence and care when applying the principles of the Law of Attraction and always stay aware of our calling to be God's example to unbelievers.

A Sovereign God Vs. Our Personal Genie

The first difference to be tackled is the secular position which claims that the universe is some kind of cosmic genie, waiting and willing to grant a person's every wish and desire. Secular experts focus on achieving material gains without thought or attention to using the law to help others or for a higher purpose.

Don't get me wrong, many secular proponents are very generous people. But in their teachings, the emphasis is placed on obtaining material things: cars, big houses, and of course, money. This worldly approach can turn Christians off. The material emphasis leaves them feeling that it is wrong or sinful to use the Law of Attraction.

"For I know the plans I have for you," declares the Lord, "plans to prosper you and not to harm you, plans to give you hope and a future." (Jeremiah 29:11)

What we as Christians often forget is that God loves us, and wants the best for us. In fact, he has already envisioned and planned out our "absolute best," which is often far better than we could ever dream or imagine.

As Christians, we know that God is not a genie, and our will is not necessarily his will. God is sovereign (e.g. possessing ultimate power) and if we ask for something that isn't good for us or isn't advantageous to the common good (his will), he won't just hand it over exclaiming: *"YOUR WISH IS MY*

COMMAND!"

By the same token, God doesn't want us to be disadvantaged, either! Disadvantage hinders the promotion of His Kingdom. God loves us as His children. Just as we would love for our kids to have everything they want in life, God wants us to be happy and to realize our greatest potential and the plans He has for us.

The Bible is filled with stories of men who experienced the favor and blessings of God, both spiritually *and* materially. Read about the lives of Abraham, Solomon, and Joseph to name only a few.

At all times, the Christian's goal is to fulfill God's purpose and plan that He has for us. But, if we additionally attract a home that we love, a great car, or money in the bank, that is not a bad thing. Keep in mind that fulfilling God's calling to preach His word through all the nations does require a certain amount of money to achieve! The problems only arise when achieving the material goals becomes more important to us than becoming the person God plans for us to be.

Okay, so God, in his ultimate power, has a plan for us and he has from day one. So, as Christians, we must remember that if we are actively using the Law of Attraction to get something that God knows won't further His plan, we might not reach our goal, no matter how well we practice the Law of Attraction. God is in charge, not the law, and as Christians, we must keep that in mind.

How freeing that is for us! The secular brand of the Law of Attraction basically states that we can have *anything* we want so long as we set our thoughts towards achieving it. If we don't get it and get it quickly, there can only be one reason - *we* didn't do something right! Ouch! Talk about a guilt trip!

14

As Christians, we also know that there is something greater than the Law of Attraction at work - God's larger plan for the world and our lives. And we know that God has larger plans for us than we could ever imagine. So, if something we have been hoping to attract doesn't happen, we know that it can only mean He has something better in mind that we don't know about yet.

We Christians know that God created the Law of Attraction in the first place. So if we keep Him sovereign in all that we do, we can be confident that the law will work perfectly to achieve His plans for the world, not just for us. No, God isn't our personal genie, which is totally okay, because what God has in store is so much better than we could ever imagine...*plans to prosper and not to harm, plans for hope and a future*. This is God's wish for you!

The Need For Action

The secular representation of the Law of Attraction suggests that all you need to do to attract everything you want is to "ask" (clarify what it is you want and ask the universe to provide it to you), "believe" (remove all doubt that you will get it) and "receive" (be prepared for it to drop into your lap).

While a certain level of credence can be given to those principles, what is left out is the biblical (and natural) notion of sowing and reaping.

Secular proponents often quote Galatians 6:7 (*a man reaps what he sows*) to support their concept that what you think about, happens. And that is indeed true.

However, this limited view of the concept of sowing and

reaping leaves out the very important fact that (in modern terms) **you can't get something for nothing**. Newton's 3rd Law of Motion states: "for every *action* there is an equal and opposite *reaction*." God's Word preaches the same principals.

Consider Jesus' "Parable of the Talents" found in Matthew 25: 14-30. In this story, a rich man left on a trip and entrusted his assets to three of his servants. He asked them to take care of them while he was gone. Two of the servants immediately *took action* to invest the money, while the third was afraid to take a risk and chose to do nothing. When the master returned, he rewarded the first two servants for their actions and punished the third.

The Bible is full of directives from God that action is always preferable to inaction:

"What good is it, my brothers, if someone says he has faith but does not have works? Can that faith save him? If a brother or sister is poorly clothed and lacking in daily food, and one of you says to them, 'Go in peace, be warmed and filled,' without giving them the things needed for the body, what good is that? So also faith by itself, if it does not have works, is dead." (James 2:14-17)

"Therefore, preparing your minds for action, and being sober-minded, set your hope fully on the grace that will be brought to you at the revelation of Jesus Christ." (1 Peter 1:13)

"Whatever you do, work heartily, as for the Lord and not for men, knowing that from the Lord you will receive the inheritance as your reward. You are serving the Lord Christ." (Colossians 3:23-24)

"Tell me what you think about this: There was a man who had two sons. He went to the first son and said, 'Son, go and work today in the vineyard.' The son answered, 'I will not go.' But later he decided he should go, and he went. Then the father went to the other son and said, 'Son, go

and work today in the vineyard.' He answered, 'Yes, sir, I will go and work.' But he did not go. Which of the two sons obeyed his father?" The Jewish leaders answered, "The first son." (Matthew 21:28-31)

"Hearing God's teaching and doing nothing is like looking at your face in the mirror and doing nothing about what you saw. You go away and immediately forget how bad you looked. But when you look into God's perfect law that sets people free, pay attention to it. If you do what it says, you will have God's blessing. Never just listen to his teaching and forget what you heard." (James 1:23-25)

To recap, God is not our personal genie just waiting to give us what we want for nothing. Christians practicing the Law of Attraction must always keep in mind that God wants us to remain active participants in His plan. We'll cover some tips and techniques for taking action later in this book.

We Don't Practice the Law of Attraction Alone

The final item to note is that secular proponents often omit the simple fact that you are not practicing the Law of Attraction alone. There are other forces at work, which can undermine the very things you are hoping to attract into your life.

To be clear, I'm not talking about competition over resources. For example, if you are hoping to attract your dream house and it sells before you are able to make the purchase; it doesn't mean that the Law of Attraction doesn't work. God is a God of "more than enough," and there are plenty of dream houses to go around for everyone.

The point that I want you to understand is that there are times that the bad guys can use the Law of Attraction just as well, or maybe better, than the good guys.

How else can organized crime, Hitler's reign of power, and child abuse be explained? I refuse to believe that the victims of those awful acts became victims just because they didn't think nice enough thoughts to attract good things into their lives. No! They were victims because bad guys used the same principals with much more success.

Just as bad guys can use the laws of physics and chemistry to build bombs to hurt people, they can use the Law of Attraction to make bad things happen to good people; and they do it all the time. As Christians, we know they are being led by the ultimate bad guy, Satan himself. Spiritual warfare is alive and well in the world, and the Law of Attraction is just one of the many tools the enemy is using to win people over to his dark side.

Subtle and less obvious than we may think, the Devil works the Law of Attraction to his advantage by planting negative and non-empowering thoughts into our minds every day. The Law of Attraction is a perfect vehicle to fight God's people because it works in our minds and challenges our confidence to become all that God has planned for us. That is why Paul so strongly encourages us in Ephesians 6: 10-13 to wrap ourselves in God's strength:

"Be strong in the Lord and in his great power. Wear the full armor of God. Wear God's armor so that you can fight against the devil's clever tricks. Our fight is not against people on earth. We are fighting against the rulers and authorities and the powers of this world's darkness. We are fighting against the spiritual powers of evil in the heavenly places. That is why you need to get God's full armor. Then on the day of evil, you will be able to stand strong. And when you have finished the whole fight, you will still be standing."

More tips and strategies for fighting Satan's destructive manipulation of the Law of Attraction will be covered in later chapters.

We ALL Practice the Law of Attraction

Many Christians ask themselves questions such as: "Should I follow the Law of Attraction?" or "Can I practice the techniques of Law of Attraction and still be a follower of God?" I think those questions are completely counter-productive.

In the same way chemistry, logic, physics, weather patterns, and planetary motion exist, so too, does the Law of Attraction. It works in our lives, positively or negatively, regardless of our conscious awareness of its presence.

As Christians, the question we should ask is: "How can I use the Law of Attraction to become better equipped to discover and fulfill God's plan for my life?"

The good news is, there are techniques and strategies to better learn how to control our thoughts and use the Law of Attraction to its best advantage. God points to many of these strategies in His Word. The rest of this book will explore those methods more fully.

4
PUTTING GOD'S LAW OF ATTRACTION
TO WORK

A joyful heart is good medicine, but a crushed spirit dries up the bones.
(Proverbs 17:22)

As mentioned earlier, secular Law of Attraction proponents often teach three basic steps to attracting what you want into your life. Those steps are:

Ask
Believe
Receive

This is a good starting point for God's Law of Attraction as well. However, I believe there are a couple of interim steps between "Believe" and "Receive" that are not properly addressed by most Law of Attraction teachers. These are "Act" and "Allow."

A short background explanation is needed before we can delve into these 5 steps. In my opinion, the best description of

21

the Law of Attraction comes from Michael Losier, who states: *"You attract into your life more of whatever you are giving your focus, attention, and energy to."*

That focus could be on bad things (which are typically attracted without your awareness), or on good things (which can be deliberate or non-deliberate).

Our goal in practicing the Law of Attraction is to minimize the non-deliberate negative focus, attention, and energy and replace it with positive. This positive focus, attention, and energy will most likely *begin* as deliberate, and as you are able to successfully practice the Law of Attraction, will evolve into a combination of deliberate and non-deliberate.

Many explanations of the Law of Attraction use the term "vibration" or "vibe" to describe the negative or positive energy created by our thoughts, and you will see them here as well. You have probably heard the expression "I'm getting a bad vibe about this," when negative thoughts and energy prevail in a situation.

Where secular Law of Attraction falls short is that it often counsels you to immediately suppress any bad thought you might have and replace it with "good and happy thoughts." While this may work at times, at other times it does little more than does applying a bandage to a wound that really needs stitches.

Because God's Law of Attraction is based on a moral compass, it is important to keep in mind that bad vibes are there for a reason, and they need to be addressed. It is possible that they are misguided and *should* be replaced by more positive thoughts and vibrations. There is also the potential that they represent a bigger issue that must be dealt with in more detail, perhaps with the help of a pastor or Christian counselor.

At all times, the goal when practicing the Law of Attraction should be to *deliberately* increase the positive over the negative vibes in our lives; while at the same time addressing any root issues that negative vibrations bring to light. In that way, you will be able to attract into your life more of what you want and less of what you don't want.

5
STEP ONE: ASK

"Ask and it will be given to you; seek and you will find; knock and the door will be opened to you." (Matthew 7:7)

Can we agree that God wants us to experience the wonderful bounty of His creation rather than just endure?

If we as His people are successful, we can do more to further His Kingdom than if we are part of the problem. As 2 Corinthians 9:8 states: *"And God is able to bless you abundantly, so that in all things at all times, having all that you need, you will abound in every good work."*

God encourages us to ask Him for what we want. While not everything we ask for is part of God's plan, if we are sincere, and what we ask for is in His will for us, we will get it.

The famous 23rd Psalm declares *"the Lord is my Shepherd, I shall not want,"* and some have taken this to mean that we should be happy with what we have. Many folks, especially Christians, have deep-rooted beliefs that wanting to achieve more in life is "bad," and may confuse material greed with the ambition to be and do their best. This mindset makes it extremely difficult to focus on what it is they really want.

While the concept of "want" most definitely includes our desire for material possessions, it goes much further. People often refuse to dream big dreams for their lives, such as careers they want to explore; causes they believe in and want to contribute to; and hopes they have for their families.

This refusal to dream results in apathetic acceptance of the status quo and hidden fear of changing. In other words, we silently accept the negative vibes in our lives as normal and believe that it is all we can or should expect.

The absence of a desire and ambition to achieve great things is *not* what God wants for us. In fact, this way of thinking is proof that the enemy is alive and well in our minds today! John 10:10 tells us: *"The thief does not come except to steal, and to kill, and to destroy. I have come that they may have life and that they may have it more abundantly."*

It's time for us as God's children to accept the abundant life He wants for us and to learn that it is okay to ask!

Learning How to Ask

I hope you are convinced that it is okay to ask, but you may still be confused. After all, you've spent most of your life virtuously suppressing the desire for more, and now step one to God's Law of Attraction is telling you to ask for it! What are you supposed to ask for, anyway?

Keep in mind that you are already asking for things all day long according to the principles of the Law of Attraction.

26

Remember, whatever you put your focus, attention and energy into, is what you will attract into your life. So, if you are deliberately focusing on having a satisfying relationship with your teenager, the chances are much greater that you *will* have a satisfying relationship with him or her than if you continue to focus on what he or she is doing wrong.

And, the Law of Attraction doesn't recognize words such as don't, not, and no as things that you would just as soon keep out of your life.

Consider when you are doing an Internet search. If you were to type in "no baseball", your search results will most definitely contain all kinds of information on baseball. In the same way, by telling yourself "I don't want to fight with my son all the time," you are placing your attention on fighting with your son and that is most likely what will happen the next time you see him. To be flip, you are just *asking* for it...

Learning to ask for what we want is easy once we begin to deliberately monitor our thoughts and focus on positive desires rather than trying to eliminate the negative.

Asking Exercise

The first thing you want to do is choose something in your life that you want (or need) to change. Let's suppose you are unhappy with your job and want to find a more inspiring career.

Take out a piece of paper and briefly brainstorm things about your current job that you *don't* like. Ideally, you should be able to come up with a list of 20 or more things that you don't like about your current job. Your list may include items similar to these:

Low wages
long hours
boring work
no customer interaction
a gloomy work environment
no flexibility
hate my boss

It may seem strange that in order to attract a better job you should start with a list of things you don't like in your current job. But, remember, we are conditioned to "grin and bear it." So even if we know we want something else, we often have no idea what we really want instead. Creating a list of things we don't like about our job helps us pave the way to identifying what we really do want in our ideal job.

PLEASE remember, the Law of Attraction draws to you those things that you give attention, focus and energy. While creating the list of things that you don't like in your job; it is *critical* to not give each item a lot of attention or emotional energy.

For example, if your list included "no flexibility," don't sit there and fume over the fact that your boss didn't let you leave early last week for your child's recital. Just write "no flexibility" and immediately move on. It might be a good idea to give yourself a time limit so that you don't spend too much time thinking about any one item on your list.

Once your list is complete, get a new piece of paper, and for each thing you don't want, ask yourself what you *do* want instead.

For example, from your first list, you may create a new list that says:

28

low wages >> generous salary

long hours >> standard 8 hour work day

boring work >> interesting work that uses my creative skills

no customer interaction >> the ability to meet with customers

a gloomy work environment >> cheerful workstations with inspiring art on the walls

no flexibility >> flexible hours

hate my boss >> a boss that respects and values my work

Once your new list (things that you *do* want) is complete, destroy the old list. Now, you have a new, positive list of what you would like to ask for with respect to your new job! Where just a few minutes ago you had uncertainty, you now have the clarity you need to ask.

This process works great for a big change such as a job, and equally well whenever you feel negative vibes in a situation. For example, suppose you are continuing to struggle with your teenager. You find yourself once again bickering over trivial things, and you hear a voice in your head crying "I don't want to fight with him anymore!"

In the past, you would have been setting yourself up for more fights (remember, Law of Attraction doesn't hear don't, not, or no), but now you recognize what you don't want and immediately ask yourself: "What do I want?" Your answer will change the vibe from negative to positive and clarify what type of relationship you want between you and your teen.

The Asking step is critical in the Law of Attraction whether we are asking for something physical, or material (such as a new house) or something less tangible (such as being able to start a charity for a worthy cause). In either case, it is crucial to first clearly (briefly) identify the problem and then clarify what we do want. To get a copy of worksheets to help you through the Asking process, please visit
R50Books.com/gloabonusreg

Once your desire has been clarified, your final task is to create a positive statement about what you want. Use that statement to keep the positive vibe of what you want in your mind and your prayers. Step 2 will contain some tips and ideas for creating a good positive desire statement.

God's Law of Attraction and Asking

Now, here is where it *really* gets good! Those practicing the secular Law of Attraction will basically create their positive statement about what they want, say *"Universe, I really want this, this and this,"* and wait for a cosmic boom to exclaim "YOUR WISH IS MY COMMAND" and drop it in their lap.

We, as God's people have the distinct privilege to go in prayer to the source of all that is, was and will be. Prayer is our way to establishing a real relationship with our heavenly Father. Just as we want our kids to talk to us and ask us for what they want and need, God wants the same from us, His children.

"Whatever you ask in my name, this I will do, that the Father may be glorified in the Son. If you ask me anything in my name, I will do it." (John 14:13-14)

"Do not be anxious about anything, but in everything by prayer and supplication with thanksgiving let your requests be made known to God.

30

And the peace of God, which surpasses all understanding, will guard your hearts and your minds in Christ Jesus." (Philippians 4:6-7)

"If you believe, you will receive whatever you ask for in prayer." (Matthew 21:22)

"Therefore, I tell you, whatever you ask for in prayer, believe that you have received it, and it will be yours." (Mark 11:24)

What an honor to be able to ask in prayer! And, because we know that God wants every good thing that He has in store for us, we can pray confidently, knowing that whether the answer is "yes," "no," or "not yet," our prayers have been answered!

6
STEP TWO: BELIEVE

"If you believe, you will receive whatever you ask for in prayer." (Matthew 21:22)

The passage above from Matthew 21 suggests that, while prayer (asking) is an all important first step, belief plays an equally important role in the Law of Attraction. Belief is tough, for Christians and non-Christians alike. We may know that we want that new house, and even ask for it, but when we look at our bank account and the way our current house has depreciated in value, it's hard to believe it could ever happen.

We've been so conditioned to think that "seeing is believing." With God's Law of Attraction, the real secret is "believing is seeing."

The problem: When we surrender to belief, it feels as though we don't have any control. We belong to a society that celebrates ingenuity, resourcefulness, and creativity. Our world isn't too excited about someone who just "blindly" believes in something and feels no need to figure out how to get it done.

Yet that is exactly what the believing step is asking us to do.

Admittedly, this step can even feel counter-intuitive to Step #3 of God's Law of Attraction: "Act." But for now, I "ask" you to just "believe" that they can work together.

Psalm 37: 5 reads: *"Commit your way to the Lord; trust also in Him and He will bring it to pass."* It doesn't say that you have to figure out "how" it will come to pass, only that you trust that, through God, it will. Remember, God created everything there is. Nothing exists that He didn't make (John 1: 3). If that is true, and we really believe it, it *should* be easy to believe that nothing is impossible, even if we can't see how it could happen in the natural.

"If you have faith as small as a mustard seed, you can say to this mulberry tree, 'Be uprooted and planted in the sea,' and it will obey you."
(Luke 17:6)

Resistance and Doubt

Let's talk a little bit about "resistance." It seems so logical to try to resist the thoughts of lack, such as "I'll never be able to get a new house." After all, our thoughts are <u>all</u> important. You will find the mere act of resisting will actually give attention, focus and energy to the lack you are trying to resist; thereby attracting more of it. Believing anything is difficult when we are feeling the tug of resistance. That is why the enemy so often uses *doubt* (another code word for resistance) to circumvent God's plans.

Easy to say, hard to… well, RESIST, right?

Positive Desire Statements

Your positive desire statements from Step 1 (Asking) are the ammunition you can use to combat negative thoughts of lack and inadequacy. The *instant* you feel resistance to a negative thought or situation, dig for that positive statement and repeat it to yourself until positive vibrations overpower the negative ones.

The best way to create a number of positive desire statements in the area you are trying to improve is to use your want list created during the "Ask" step. To illustrate, in our example of trying to attract the ideal job, we created the following list of wants:

generous wages
standard 8 hour work day
interesting work that uses my creative skills
the ability to meet with customers
cheerful workstations with inspiring art on the walls
flexible hours
a boss that respects and values my work

Use these wants together with positive phrases such as "I love"; "It is exciting"; or "it feels great"; to create statements describing your ideal job situation.

For example:

"It feels great to be paid a generous wage in my ideal job that provides everything my family needs."

"I love that in my ideal job I work only 8 hours with the flexibility I need to lead a rich personal life as well."

"It is exciting to know my ideal job uses my creative skills to perform interesting, rewarding work."

"It feels great to meet and work with customers face to face in my ideal job."

Make sure to create a statement that has a positive emotional impact on you when you repeat it. Don't make your statement too complicated, as you want to be able to memorize it and repeat it at will whenever you need a positive trigger, but do include things that are meaningful to you.

For example, if you are fine-tuning your positive desire statement for a new house, and you have discovered that it is very important for that house to have a front porch, include the phrase "front porch" directly in your desire statement. Every time you say "front porch" you will have a positive boost to your emotions which will raise your vibrations.

Most Law of Attraction teachers suggests you create your positive desire statements in the present tense - for example: "I have a job where I leave on time every day." However, if you don't actually have a job where you can leave on time, you will probably have doubt and resistance surface when you say it. The doubt and resistance will likely *lower* your vibrations rather than raise them, *reducing* the level of the pure and total belief you want to achieve.

One way to combat this problem is to use the phrase "my ideal job" rather than "my job." So, rather than saying *"I have a job where I leave on time every day"*, you would rephrase it to say *"I love knowing that in my ideal job, I leave on time every day."* Those subtle changes make the positive desire statement more real to you (after all, in your ideal job, you will leave on time every day), and increase the vibrations rather than decrease them.

Another suggestion is to add the phrase "I am in the process of" to your desire statement. For example: *"I am in the process of finding my ideal job where I leave on time every day."*

This achieves two things. First, the statement becomes believable to you, rather than creating doubt. And second, you become an active participant - you are in the process of doing it. However, it doesn't describe *how* you will implement the process as you may not know how it will happen. Remember, that part is up to God. We are like a supporting actor in God's plan. But the action *is* needed, as described more fully in Step 3 of the Law of Attraction process.

To get a copy of worksheets to help you to create positive desire statements, please visit **R50Books.com/gloabonusreg**.

Declarations From God's Word

Before moving on, let's not forget those positive declarations that God has already provided to us in His Word. Declarations such as:

"I can do all things through Christ who give me strength!"
(Philippians 4:13)

"For he has rescued me from the kingdom of darkness and transferred me into the Kingdom of Christ Jesus." (Colossians 1:13)

"Because I belong to Christ I have become a new person. The old life is gone; a new life has begun!" (2 Corinthians 5:17)

"For I am God's masterpiece. He has created me anew in Christ Jesus, so I can do the good things he planned for me long ago."
(Ephesians 2:10)

"No, despite all these things, overwhelming victory is mine through Christ, who loves me." (Romans 8:37)

There are hundreds of other positive declarations in God's Word that can help us to overcome doubt and resistance and promote our belief. These positive declarations should become part of our daily arsenal when seeking to positively use the Law of Attraction.

Visualize and Emotionalize

In addition to having positive declarations at the ready to create belief, many people have found it effective to find additional, personalized ways to visualize and emotionalize their positive desire statements. In other words, really tune into the way you will think, feel, and act once you have received what you desire.

All people are wired differently, and every person reacts emotionally to different triggers. These triggers can be visual, verbal, or sensual (touch and feel).

Your verbal triggers are activated every time you use one of your positive declarations, especially if you take the time to write declarations that appeal to your emotions, and speak them aloud. Favorite music and inspiring books are another way to use verbal triggers to keep your positive vibrations flowing and reduce resistance and doubt.

Sitting down and writing a lengthy version of your desire statement, which describes the who, what, where, when and how of what you want is another great way to use verbal triggers to increase your level of belief.

Another popular tool for visualizing your desires is to

38

create a vision board with pictures. In this method, you use a scrapbook or large poster board to paste pictures, phrases, and other reminders of what you want out of life. By spending time creating your vision board and looking at it daily, your belief that you will achieve your wants will increase; with resistance and doubt fading away.

If you respond more to touch and feel, you may want to focus on how having what you want will affect your senses - what does it smell like, feel like, and taste like? Try to add this information to your descriptions and pictures in order to use those sensual triggers to increase belief and remove doubt.

If you are hoping to attract your ideal career, you may want to create a vision board that shows a picture of you leaving an attractive workspace with a prominent clock showing the time as 5:00. You may prefer to write a detailed description of your ideal work situation. You could also find some music that triggers emotions regarding your ideal career, or maybe find something you can touch that will make you think about it.

Regardless of the method you prefer, the goal is to see and feel all of the little details - the more details the better. Really get into it and open up the power of your emotions - feel the joy and excitement when receiving or accomplishing what you desire.

It is probably a good time to remind you again that, although many times discussion about the Law of Attraction leads to talk of material things, material gain is only the tip of what can be accomplished through using these powerful principles. Go wild for God in visualizing everything you could accomplish for His Kingdom.

To get resources to help you to visualize your goals, please visit**R50Books.com/gloabonusreg**

7
STEP THREE: ACT

"You will always harvest what you plant." (Luke 6:7)

We may have asked God for what we want in prayer. We believe that God can do all things, but many of us may have trouble believing fully enough to just wait for it to happen in God's time. Instead, we try to bend the situation to make it happen faster or in the way that we want - rather than to just release it to God's will.

We are in good company. God had promised Abraham and Sarah that they would have a son, but the years passed and...no son. Sarah was getting older and older, and still, no son. Finally, the couple decided to take matters into their own hands rather than to be patient and wait for God's promise.

Sarah allowed Abraham to sleep with her maid, Hagar, who became pregnant and had a boy, named Ishmael. The story in Genesis tells us, however, that Ishmael was not the son God had intended for Abraham. In time, Sarah did become pregnant and had a son, Isaac. Because God loved Abraham

41

and kept his promise, it turned out for the best, but who knows how much sooner Abraham and Sarah may have realized God's best for them if they hadn't tried to manipulate things on their own.

"For who knows a person's thoughts except that person's own spirit within? In the same way, no one knows the thoughts of God except the Spirit of God." (1 Corinthians 2:11)

One Thing a Day

Before anyone gets confused, Abraham and Sarah's attempt to speed up God's promise is NOT the Action needed for God's Law of Attraction. We can't imagine God's best - and any attempt on our part to speed things along will only confuse the situation. It doesn't pay to waste our time trying to figure out how God will work things out, so stop worrying about it!

But, just as the master in the story of the three servants (Matthew 25: 14-30) expected his servants to take action and invest his assets while he was gone; so too God expects us to prepare ourselves for the good things to come into our lives.

For example, if we have asked for a new car, it is not enough to merely believe that a new, fully loaded Lexus will drop out of the sky onto our driveway. The chances of that happening are mighty slim.

But, if in belief, we begin saving a portion of our salary for a down payment, and visit car lots to test drive different models, God will eventually work through these actions to make a car that we like available at terms we can afford.

In order to attract your ideal career, you should take the positive action of preparing a great resume and spreading the word to trustworthy associates that you would be open to new opportunities. God will provide the opening, but your participation is needed to take advantage of it.

Sometimes a want is so big is seems that any action on our part is just a drop in the ocean. In those cases, taking no action often becomes our easiest choice.

If you have a goal that you truly feel God is calling you to achieve, you should commit to doing, at least, one thing each day toward achieving it. The one thing doesn't have to be big at all. Maybe it is just a matter of reading a bit in a trade journal for your ideal career field or fine-tuning your resume or calling an associate you haven't talked to in a while.

Provided that you aren't trying to control the situation over God, a little action is always better than no action. First, it helps remove doubt and resistance to your goal. Second, it is a way to respond to God's call with belief. You may have no idea how your little action will help you to achieve a seemingly impossible goal, but God can do the impossible.

The difference between God's Law of Attraction and the secular version is that in the secular law the "universe" makes it happen, but God works through us and wants us to act.

Discerning God's Will

Sometimes, our only action in a situation is to be able to discern what God is asking us to do. Once we know His will for our lives and just go with the flow, rather than worrying it to death or trying to manipulate the situation, He can achieve all the great things he has in store for us. Remember, God does have plans for you. In Jeremiah 29:11 we're told: *"For I know the plans I have for you," declares the Lord, "plans to prosper you and not to harm you, plans to give you hope and a future."*

It would be so great if God's will were like a fortune cookie where you ask a question: "Is this guy my ideal mate?" open the fortune and get the answer. But, you probably already know God doesn't operate like that at all. Even though we may be card-carrying Christians, there is no guarantee we will be able to spot God's will when we see it. Fortunately, God *has* given us a number of tools to help us to better discern His will for our lives.

First, God *wants* to have a close relationship with us. Do you have someone - your spouse or a best friend - with whom you are so close that you can finish their sentences and sense their moods even when others cannot? The reason you are so close to this person is because you have taken the time to cultivate a true relationship with him or her. By building such a close relationship, you grew to be able to discern things about the person that other people do not recognize.

In the same way, as we take the time to develop a close relationship with God, the better we will get at discerning His will.

Second, the Bible is God's greatest tool to help us discern His will. In Psalm 119:105, David tells the Lord: *"Your word is a lamp to my feet and a light for my path."* By reading and studying God's Word, we are able to strengthen our relationship with Him, which further helps us to discern God's will for us.

"Don't worry about anything; instead, pray about everything. Tell God what you need, and thank him for all he has done." (Philippians 4:6)

Next, God has given us the power of prayer to directly ask Him whenever we need his guidance and direction: *"If you need wisdom, ask our generous God, and he will give it to you. He will not rebuke you for asking." (James 1:5).* We never have to worry about asking a dumb question or feeling unworthy to ask God for what we need and want. God wants us to pray about everything - as that is our main form of communication with Him!

Finally, God has given us counselors to help us to discern His will for us. These counselors come in natural form; through advice from trusted mentors and through the Holy Spirit (which can be felt in any number of ways, but is often described as our conscience).

"And this righteousness will bring peace. Yes, it will bring quietness and confidence forever." (Isaiah 32:17)

Ultimately, when following God's will for our lives, despite the actual circumstances of the moment, we will feel a peace. When trying to decide between two choices, slowing down and seeing which choice gives a greater feeling of peace makes sense. That choice will most likely be God's will.

Daily Practice

Another action of note is the mere act of daily practicing God's Law of Attraction in our lives. Our goal should be to be able to keep positive vibrations flowing more often than negative vibrations, but this isn't something that just happens overnight.

We can only focus on a small amount of what we actually do each day, and the rest we do pretty much on auto-pilot. We don't have to deliberately think about how to get to work in the morning or how to brush our teeth. We have done these things so often they become involuntary to us.

Satan is busy planting negative thoughts and emotions into our subconscious which lowers our vibrations. We don't know this is happening, we just see the results. Our goal, as we practice God's Law of Attraction, is to *deliberately* combat these negative thoughts and emotions and increase the positive vibrations. We have to keep at the deliberate intent until it becomes an involuntary habit.

Deliberately changing anything of real value takes time, and we must be committed *every day* to deliberately work God's Law of Attraction in our lives. At some point, the struggle to replace negative vibes with positive ones will lessen and become more involuntary. But, because Satan is always looking for new ways to keep us from God's best, we will always have new challenges to overcome.

In God's Law of Attraction, it isn't enough to just "ask", "believe" and "receive." Action on our part is an important ingredient in attracting the good things God has in store for us. In addition to actively working to discern God's will in our lives, we also need to take the actions needed to set the wheels of our desire into process. An especially important action is Step 4 in God's Law of Attraction process: to *allow* what you are attracting into your life.

8
STEP FOUR: ALLOW

"Commit your actions to the Lord, and your plans will succeed."
(Proverbs 16:3)

Regardless of how much you ask, believe, or act, the Law of Attraction can still go "wrong" if you fail to achieve Step 4 of the process, which is to <u>allow</u> what you are attracting into your life. Most of the time we do not consciously reject the attraction of these things, but we are not typically allowing them to happen in our life, either.

To explain, imagine a young man is attending a seminar on a topic that is brand new to him, but could open up a lot of career opportunities in the future. He is very excited about the seminar and hopes he will learn a lot.

One of the presenters is particularly interesting and motivating, and by the morning break, this young man is excited and inspired to further explore what the speaker described.

The young man sees the presenter packing up his presentation materials and thinks he'd really love to talk to him further about his speech and get some advice on next steps he could take.

At this stage in the scenario, he could do one of several things:

First, he could turn and leave the room, telling himself that the speaker is way too busy to give him any of his time. And anyway, he can just research the topic some more on the Internet or read a few more books on the subject instead of bothering the man for more of his time.

His second choice would be to hang back in his seat, watching the presenter pack up and hope he turns, catches his eye and strikes up a conversation. That way, he is really just leaving it all up to fate - whatever will be will be.

This young man's third option would be to approach the man confidently, offer to help him pack up his gear and strike up a conversation about the parts of his presentation he found most interesting.

Which way should the young man go? The outcome of his seminar experience will be completely different depending on the choice he makes.

God's Law of Attraction works similarly to the above scenario. Let's say that you really want to change your career. You have defined specific desires related to your ideal career (ask). You have created a strong positive desire statement and created other visualization techniques (believe). You've written your resume and tentatively sent out feelers to your friends and colleagues that you might be interested in a new career (act).

Congratulations! You have achieved probably 80% more toward your goal than most people already. But, you are only part way there, as you still need to "allow" your ideal career into your life.

Will you choose scenario 1, losing yourself in research over the best companies to work for, not really expecting that you will ever actually be able to take the plunge and leave your current job?

Will you hover on the edges, talking about someday and waiting for the ideal job to turn around, notice you and invite you in?

Or will you actively allow new opportunities into your life with confidence and enthusiasm?

What keeps people from actually allowing the things they want into their lives? There are two factors that are most common: doubt and limiting beliefs.

Doubt

"But when you ask, you must believe and not doubt, because the one who doubts is like a wave of the sea, blown and tossed by the wind."
(James 1:6)

The first thing that will prevent you from allowing your desires into your life is the presence of doubt. If you recall in Part 2 of the process (Believing), resistance to believing something will happen is caused by the doubt that we carry. And, the presence of doubt causes negative vibrations, a popular ploy by the enemy to circumvent God's plans.

Satan does this in a subtle way we often don't even

recognize as doubt. We may see it as common sense. For example, let's say you desire a bigger house closer to the schools your children attend. You are open to the Law of Attraction, so you create a positive desire statement and a vision board to describe some of the things you want in your new house.

You have prayed to God and believe he supports your desire for a new house. You have researched the areas you might want to live in and started to put a little away each paycheck. In other words, you have "asked", "believed", and "acted".

Then, the enemy begins to implant that small seed of doubt. You look at the amount you are able to save each month and calculate how long it will take to get a down-payment. You look at the real estate market in your current neighborhood and think there is no way you will be able to sell your house for what you need in order to make a move.

As the enemy plants the seeds of doubt, you respond by resisting the idea that you could ever have a new home. You may even start to feel guilty for desiring something so far out of your realm. You start to justify why your current situation isn't all that bad. And Satan does a happy dance as you disallow that new house right out of possibility.

Doubt has its evil brother, "worry," right by its side, too. Instead of doubting something good will ever happen, worry instead works on our fear that bad things will happen. For example, you worry that you might lose your job after moving to a new home and won't be able to meet the bills. The enemy loves worry as much as doubt because either one can change the vibrational flow from positive to negative in the blink of an eye. That's all he needs to keep you from achieving God's best.

God is a God That Can Do the Impossible

You see, what the enemy tries to keep you from remembering, is that God is a God that can do the impossible. Remember the Bible Story right after Jesus fed 5,000 people with just a little bread and a couple of fish?

Well, after that happened, the disciples set out in a boat, leaving Jesus behind to pray. After a while, they were pretty far out and it was getting dark and windy. They saw Jesus walking toward them on the water but thought it was a ghost. Well, that freaked them out, for sure. But Peter, always the adventurer, said to Jesus, *"If that's really you, can I do that too?"*

"Come on," Jesus replied and reached out his hands to Peter. Tentatively, Peter left the boat and began walking on the water to Jesus.

How cool was that? How excited he must have been! Walking on water - something that is completely impossible for man to do. But, Jesus made it happen. You would think that would be enough to convince everyone, right?

But what happened? Peter took his eyes off of Jesus, looked at the waves, and the enemy was able to plant the seeds of doubt and worry. Instantly, Peter crashed into the waves, floundering for his life.

Now here's the good part. *"Help me!"* Peter cried, and Jesus once again reached out his hand and helped him up. He didn't say "Well, if you don't want my help, just get yourself out of the water." No, he reached out his hand and saved him. *"You of little faith,"* He said, *"Why did you doubt?"* I'm sure Peter was wondering the same thing! Read Matthew 14: 22-31 for the entire story.

Our God is a God that can do the impossible, *and* a God of second chances. With those two things on our side, there is no room left for doubt or worry in our lives!

Limiting Beliefs

The second thing that can keep you from allowing your wants to be attracted into your life is, as Tony Robbins says, "your story as to why you can't get them." Others call this story your *limiting beliefs*.

"Stay alert! Watch out for your great enemy, the devil. He prowls around like a roaring lion, looking for someone to devour." (1 Peter 5:8)

There are a lot of definitions for limiting beliefs, but in a nutshell, a limiting belief is something that you believe to be true about yourself that really is not true; and it prevents you from moving forward as you'd like. A limiting belief is often centered on an attribute or circumstance that you think will keep you from achieving your wants, such as your age or income.

The enemy loves to use your limiting beliefs against you, especially if you are on the road to realizing God's plans. Remember, the closer you get to God and His plans for you, the harder Satan will work to keep you from reaching your destiny.

You can start to notice your limiting beliefs by paying attention to when you hear yourself saying "not," "no," "don't," or "can't." For example:

"I'm not social enough to be a good salesman."
"I'm not thin enough to find my ideal partner."

"I can't speak in public."
"I don't know enough."
"I'm not good enough."
"I can't hang onto money."

The list can go on and on. Often, these limiting beliefs have subconsciously been with us since we were children. We may have heard our parents or other important adults say them about themselves or about us, and they have stuck with us; even though we are not consciously aware of the thoughts or that they are hurting us. So even though we have dreams of better things, those dreams are often stifled by our limiting beliefs.

The first step in overcoming our limiting beliefs and allowing room for our dreams is to begin noticing what those limiting beliefs are. Then, we need to take conscious action to overcome those beliefs and replace them with new, empowering beliefs. Here are some techniques to do that:

1. **Choose to stop agreeing**. Ultimately our thoughts are our thoughts and although we might have believed the lie of limiting beliefs in the past, we can choose to stop believing them now.

The past does not equal the future and we can start changing our future today by remembering that we are children of God, made in His image. And remember, God doesn't make junk.

"For we are God's masterpiece. He has created us anew in Christ Jesus, so we can do the good things he planned for us long ago."
(Ephesians 2:10)

Although the enemy would prefer we forget that, we can start to take charge right now, today, and claim the wonderful things God has in store for us by choosing to stop agreeing with those limiting beliefs.

2. **Pay attention**. Once you have chosen to stop accepting your limiting beliefs, you need to start noticing what those limiting beliefs are and when they plague you the most. Figuring this out is key to making a change.

You've got to pay attention. When you pay attention to where your mind is drifting when you're "not thinking about anything," you will start to uncover your limiting beliefs. You will be able to identify them because they will seem to just spin round and round, building upon each other, crowding out your peace and joy. Job 27:20 says: *"Terrors overtake him like a flood; a tempest steals him away in the night."* Those are the beliefs the enemy is using to keep you from allowing God's blessings into your life.

3. **Question your beliefs**. The next step is to challenge those limiting beliefs when you have them. Approach them as though you were a "know-it-all" teenager arguing with his or her parents. For example, suppose your limiting beliefs tell you that you are too old to find your ideal mate. Challenge that belief with questions such as: "Has anyone my age ever found their ideal mate? How often? Isn't it possible that I could do it too? Who says I'm too old?"

Doubt and resistance may just cave right there to your persistent, badgering questions against the limiting beliefs.

4. **Test your assumptions**. You've heard the phrases "act as if," and "fake it 'til you make it," and now is your chance to give it a try. You have identified a limiting belief and challenged it to a point where you have at least lowered your doubt and resistance; now it's time to get your big toe wet and start to wade into the unknown.

Sign up for a singles event at church or strike up a conversation with someone you find interesting. Whether it goes as planned or not, ask the question: "Did I survive?"

Since the answer is "yes" (or you wouldn't be around to answer the question), you can be sure that your past limiting beliefs about the subject are really just a story you've been telling yourself. Intend to build a new story for your life, as God's amazing child.

5. **Change your thoughts**. Now, it's time to change those negative thoughts and beliefs into positive declarations. Instead of "I'm too old to find love and get married," say "my best years are still to come - I am a child of God and He will lead me to my ideal mate." Instead of "I'm not good enough," say "I am God's masterpiece and I can do all things through Christ who gives me strength!"

Start building your arsenal of positive declarations and affirmations. Memorize your positive affirmations and repeat them over and over in the car or on your daily walk. Embed them into your subconscious so that when the enemy strikes with a negative limiting belief, you have the ammunition to crush those thoughts with positive, God affirming truths.

Give yourself time to embed these new thoughts. You've had years to fine-tune your limiting beliefs, and as impatient as you are to replace them, it will take some time to do so. Experts agree it takes a minimum of 21-28 days to create a new habit. In order to create new beliefs about yourself, you will need at least this much time, or more. Be persistent, and you will be successful.

It Isn't All Or Nothing

One final thought on allowing God's blessings into your life through His Law of Attraction. We are often led to believe that according to the Law of Attraction "whatever we think about, we create." True to a point, but Napoleon Hill puts it better by stating *"Whatever you believe, you can achieve."* Just thinking a negative *thought* once or twice won't cause a negative *belief.*

There is a tremendous amount of pressure to never think a negative thought under the first assumption, and we Christians just love trying to be perfect. So the minute we think a negative thought, we feel we have failed.

The truth is one little thought does not have all that much power. The power comes from thinking the same thought over and over again until it's a belief. The more you think a thought and believe it, the more it affects your vibration. This vibration is what attracts. The Law of Attraction responds to your vibration, not the words you've said or thought (although notice that your words and thoughts *can* affect your vibration).

Just as you need time to embed your positive affirmations into your wiring, one negative thought is not going to cause a limiting belief and make bad things happen to you. It is a series of negative thoughts over time that creates your limiting beliefs. So the key to "allowing" is to reduce the number of your negative thoughts and increase the positive one. 100% compliance is not required. Even a small decrease in your negative thoughts will increase your vibration and reduce the doubt and resistance you feel.

9
STEP FIVE: RECEIVE

"Give thanks in all circumstances; for this is the will of God in Christ Jesus for you." (1 Thessalonians 5:18)

The final step in God's Law of Attraction process is to receive His blessings into your life. Remember that regardless of whether good things or bad are happening in your life the Law of Attraction has taken place. The purpose of learning to use the Law of Attraction is to intentionally work Steps 1-4 in order to allow more blessings into your life and less bad things.

It may seem like the final step, to "Receive," is a bit anti-climactic because usually you receive what you have attracted without band music, confetti and parades. It just happens. If you are not aware of God and His Law of Attraction at work, you might not even appreciate it for what it is.

Rather than use the word "receive," it might make more sense to say our goal in Step 5 is to "recognize." Recognize what the Law of Attraction has brought into your life, andwhere (or from whom) those blessings came from in the first place.

What makes the Law of Attraction great is gratitude for your blessings. Don't forget Who gives all good things. There is not much joy and peace when a blessing is received with a sense of entitlement rather than genuine gratitude for what you have.

Here is a great story of God's Law of Attraction truly at work. My husband's car was really on its last leg. With 150,000+ miles on it, it leaked oil, needed a new timing belt any day, and was tilting on 4 bald tires. We were spending money right and left on its repairs, and it wasn't safe to drive our family around in. As much as he loved it - we knew we needed a new car soon.

We both really hate the car buying experience and were not keen on most of the used cars we'd seen, so we just put it off week after week.

One day, my husband was playing around with a new goal setting tool and selected "get a new car" as his goal. He described the color (black), the tinted windows, and the four-wheel drive. When the tool asked *when* he wanted the car, he laughed and wrote "this Saturday." (These actions satisfied the "Ask and Believe" steps as he clearly identified what he wanted and visualized it as he wrote the descriptive statements of what the car would be like.)

Friday night of that same week, I noticed a big event at a used car lot on my way home from work. I typically don't even notice that kind of stuff while I'm driving, but maybe it was the cheerleading team dancing on the sidewalk in front that caught my eye. For some reason, I picked up my cell phone, called my husband and asked if he wanted to check it out (I didn't know anything about his goal setting exercise at this point).

He laughed and said "Sure, why not, after all, we will probably never get a car if we don't start looking at cars, right?" Not to mention I could tell the prospect of cheerleaders intrigued him quite a bit. (This satisfies the "Action" step of the process.)

As we walked through the lot, I had in my head the year and models that we could add to our budget comfortably. Unfortunately, most of those didn't fit with my husband's vision of the car he wanted. He kept walking back to a current year SUV: 4X4, black, tinted windows, everything.

The salesman walking the lot with us smelled our interest and ran in to get the keys. The test drive was great! Infact, we learned the mileage was under 1,000 because someone had purchased the car and returned it to trade-up just a few weeks later. (Taking the test drive satisfied the "Allow" step of the process, as we suspended our limiting beliefs long enough to allow the Law of Attraction to work.)

Long story short, we were able to get the car my husband had envisioned and even better, we were able to get it used with super low mileage and a warranty still in place. We got it at the price I was willing to pay. AND, we got it by Saturday.

I wish I could say that the car lot magically got us through the paperwork process in under an hour, but then again, it wasn't a Disney movie. Even so, I'd say God's Law of Attraction was working quite well, and my husband and I both joyfully completed Step 5 by thanking God for his blessing.

10
OVERCOMING COMMON CHALLENGES TO GOD'S LAW OF ATTRACTION

"Know Him in all your paths, and He will keep your ways straight"
(Proverbs 3:6)

Secular Law of Attraction gurus will teach you that getting everything you want in life is as easy as "ask, believe and receive." By now, you probably understand that it's not quite so cut and dried.

We all have hidden feelings and beliefs that cause negative vibrational flow, and prevent us from acting on our instincts and allowing good things to happen to us. As Christians, we can understand that the enemy uses these hidden feelings and beliefs to his benefit by preventing us from fully embracing God's plan for our lives. While we touched on this already in prior sections of this book, a few areas warrant some extra attention.

Guilt

Guilt is the ultimate spiritual warfare tactic used by Satan to create resistance and negative vibrational pull. We can feel guilty about almost everything. We have too much money. We want too much money. We are successful. We aren't successful. We messed up - again. We aren't good enough. We aren't worthy.

It is so important to remove the resistance and negative vibrational pull that guilt creates *as fast as you can*. And, as Christians, we have one quiver in our bow that secular Law of Attraction practitioners don't. We *know* that we are saved by *grace*, not by being good enough, or behaving in the right way. Jesus already shouldered all our mess-ups and our hang-ups. We are God's precious children, His masterpiece. And throughout every day, every hour, every second we have a new chance and a new beginning.

Guilt comes in two forms: warranted (you sinned and now feel bad about it) and unwarranted (you have negative limiting beliefs that lead you to think you are not good enough for some reason). Either way, the solution is to take it to God, confess your sin or doubt and accept his forgiveness and grace.

The fact is: we don't have to erase guilt completely from our lives to overcome the enemy. We can turn Satan's goal around by using guilt as a positive tool to bring us back to God. When we sense that guilty feeling creep into the pit of our stomach, we only have to recognize the reason for the guilt, confess it to Christ Jesus, and accept his grace and forgiveness. Positive vibrations are the result!

Money is the root of all evil

Material desire is an area where Christians struggle big time with embracing the Law of Attraction. Part of it stems from the fact that the secular law, which receives most of the media attention, preaches a selfish, material use for the law above all else. You *can* have the car, the house, the boat, the jewelry you've always desired, and you can do it *debt-free!* Kind of like a cheesy late night infomercial, this appeal to our self-indulgent side is offending (and, might I venture, a little scary) to a lot of Christians.

Can we agree, however, that to further God's kingdom here on earth we need physical resources? Have you been to church lately where they haven't taken a collection? Isn't a big part of a missionary organization's job to raise funds? And haven't you felt just a little bit *guilty* (there's that word again) that you couldn't do more for these causes?

Often misquoted, 1 Timothy 6:10 declares: *"For the love of money is the root of all kinds of evil."* Not money itself, merely the love of it above all else. We should love the Lord above all else (Matthew 22: 37), but having money won't prevent us from doing that. In fact, Jesus himself knew the benefits of having money - His disciple Matthew, Zaccheus and Joseph of Arimathea were all wealthy and had prominent places in Jesus' ministry. Joseph even donated the land to bury Jesus after he was crucified. There are many rich men in the Bible who were favored by God: Abraham, Isaac, Jacob, David, Solomon, Jehoshaphat, and more.

Probably the best way to describe how money might negatively affect our relationship with Christ is the concept that our hearts have a pre-built-in space in which Jesus wants to live, and he won't live in any other space. That space is reserved to house our *most important allegiance.*

If there is something else in that space, Jesus can't live there. That "something else" is often material possessions, but can be anything: a girlfriend or boyfriend, our profession, or even exercise or another hobby.

There is room for these things if they are kept in the right perspective with what is the most important - or rather, kept in some other space than Jesus' space. Jesus wants our commitment and that special space in our hearts. Money is just one thing that could get in the way if we start seeing it as more important than God's plans for us and the world.

Fear

After guilt, fear might be the enemy's favorite weapon to keep people from experiencing God's best. Everyone has experienced fear of failure to some degree. This is doubt in our ability to achieve what we want, caused by our limiting beliefs.

Remember, limiting beliefs are basically our story to ourselves about why we cannot get the things we want in life, and are centered on attributes about ourselves that we think get in the way, such as "I'm too old." These limiting beliefs create fear that if we do open up to receive God's best, we will fail. The result is our personal choice to fail.

But did you know that Satan is so clever that he also embeds a fear of success into us? What in the world is that?

The fear of success often does not arrive until you are moving forward and genuinely seeing things happen towards your goal. But you are not there yet, so visualization takes over and your inner mind starts to fill in the unknowns of how your life will be in your unfamiliar future.

The enemy smells victory because you don't know what to expect and he is more than willing to fill in the blanks for you.

Suppose you have followed all of the steps to God's Law of Attraction to achieve your ideal career, and you have just started a new job with much more potential for growth within the company. In order to get your new job, you tackled many of your limiting beliefs. Satan realizes he cannot work through those limiting beliefs anymore. So, now he has to find a new strategy to foil God's plan for you.

You don't know a lot of people in your new job and feel a little lonely. The enemy grabs onto that feeling and builds it until you begin to believe that if you continue to pursue your ideal career, you will be lonely for the rest of your life. Fearing lifelong loneliness, you unconsciously start to sabotage your career efforts.

On paper, it seems almost incredible, but Satan uses this subtle tactic all the time to mess with our minds and keep us off track. We have to remember, God's plan is for us to be fulfilled and serving Him in all areas of our life. If we trust Him, we have nothing to fear.

How do we overcome our fears? Go to God! His word constantly reminds us that He is our source of strength and courage:

"So be strong and courageous! Do not be afraid and do not panic before them. For the Lord your God will personally go ahead of you. He will neither fail you nor abandon you." (Deuteronomy 31:6)

Impatience

The world we live in is committed to instant gratification. And the secular law of attraction feeds on peoples' desire to change their lives instantly. But the truth of God's Law of Attraction is that, while God can create miracles in a moment, most of the time we have to be patient and wait for His plan to unfold:

"Consider the farmers who patiently wait for the rains in the fall and in the spring. They eagerly look for the valuable harvest to ripen. You, too, must be patient. Take courage, for the coming of the Lord is near." (James 5:7-8)

There are many things that could be creating negative vibrational pull and delaying your success. Maybe you can clarify your positive desire statement to more clearly identify your want or find some additional ways to visualize your desire. You might want to work on removing any remaining doubt and resistance you may still have, and identify any limiting beliefs that may be holding you back from allowing your desire into your life.

But these tactics may still not speed things along. As the priest said in the movie "Rudy": *"Prayer is something we do in our time. The answers come in God's time."*

Ultimately, the answer is as simple as letting go of your control and re-committing your desire to God through prayer. Quit worrying or even thinking about how things will get done and let God handle the 'how.'

"Can all your worries add a single moment to your life?"
(Matthew 6:27)

God is the architect and creator of His Law of Attraction, and it will work whether you are aware of it or not. What you focus your energy and attention on will be created in your life, and, like all things, as Christians, our only task is to have faith and commit our lives to Christ.

"Commit your actions to the Lord and your plans will succeed."
(Proverbs 16:3

11
FOLLOW THE STEPS AND ACHIEVE GOD'S BEST!

For there is a proper time and procedure for every matter, though a person may be weighed down by misery. (Ecclesiastes 8:6)

I hope it is now clear that the Law of Attraction is not a menacing new age threat to God's way, but rather a natural law put in place by God Himself to help us to achieve all that He has in store for us!

It is by no means as easy or as cut and dried as secular proponents of the Law of Attraction will lead you to believe. Satan's relentless attack on our thoughts and emotions and commitment to making us believe we can't achieve our goals is evidence that God's Law of Attraction is strong stuff.

Practicing the five steps to God's Law of Attraction day after day helps keep us focused on Him and His plans for us and does increase the positive results we see happening in our lives.

Here are God's Five Steps one last time explained better than I ever could, straight from His Word:

Step 1: Ask

"Keep on asking, and you will receive what you ask for. Keep on seeking, and you will find. Keep on knocking, and the door will be opened to you." (Matthew 7:7)

"If you need wisdom, ask our generous God, and he will give it to you. He will not rebuke you for asking." (James 1:5)

"Do not be anxious about anything, but in every situation, by prayer and petition, with thanksgiving, present your requests to God." (Philippians 4:6)

"As soon as I pray, you answer me; you encourage me by giving me strength." (Psalm 138:3)

"If you believe, you will receive whatever you ask for in prayer." (Matthew 21:22)

"You can ask for anything in my name, and I will do it so that the Son can bring glory to the Father. Yes, ask me for anything in my name, and I will do it!" (John 14:13-14)

Step 2: Believe

"The Lord answered, "If you had faith even as small as a mustard seed, you could say to this mulberry tree, 'May you be uprooted and thrown into the sea,' and it would obey you!" (Luke 17:6)

"I tell you the truth, you can say to this mountain, May you be lifted up and thrown into the sea,' and it will happen. But you must really believe it will happen and have no doubt in your heart." (Mark 11:23)

"Jesus looked at them intently and said, 'Humanly speaking, it is

70

impossible. But with God everything is possible.'" (Matthew 19:36)

"Then he touched their eyes and said, 'Because of your faith, it will happen.'" (Matthew 9:29)

"Words are powerful; take them seriously. Words can be your salvation. Words can also be your damnation." (Matthew 12:37)

"It is written: 'I believed; therefore I have spoken. Since we have that same spirit of faith, we also believe and therefore speak.'" (2 Corinthians 4:13)

Step 3: Act

"Give and you will receive. Your gift will return to you in full— pressed down, shaken together to make room for more, running over, and poured into your lap. The amount you give will determine the amount you get back." (Luke 6:38)

"You will always harvest what you plant." (Luke 6:7)

"Lazy people are soon poor; hard workers get rich." (Proverbs 10:4)

"You can make this choice by loving the Lord your God, obeying him, and committing yourself firmly to him. This is the key to your life. And if you love and obey the Lord, you will live long in the land the Lord swore to give your ancestors Abraham, Isaac, and Jacob." (Deuteronomy 30:30)

"Whether you turn to the right or to the left, your ears will hear a voice behind you, saying, 'This is the way; walk in it.'" (Isaiah 30:21)

Step 4: Allow

"For I can do everything through Christ, who gives me strength." (Philippians 4:13)

"Don't let evil conquer you, but conquer evil by doing good." (Romans 12:21)

"Commit your actions to the Lord, and your plans will succeed." (Proverbs 16:3)

"If you need wisdom, ask our generous God, and he will give it to you. He will not rebuke you for asking." (James 1:5)

"Can any one of you by worrying add a single hour to your life?" (Matthew 6:27)

"Cast all your anxiety on him because he cares for you." (1 Peter 5:7)

"The temptations in your life are no different from what others experience. And God is faithful. He will not allow the temptation to be more than you can stand. When you are tempted, he will show you a way out so that you can endure."
(1 Corinthians 10:13)

"That is why I tell you not to worry about everyday life—whether you have enough food and drink, or enough clothes to wear. Isn't life more than food, and your body more than clothing? Look at the birds. They don't plant or harvest or store food in barns, for your heavenly Father feeds them. And aren't you far more valuable to him than they are?" (Matthew 6: 25-26)

Step 5: Receive

"You can pray for anything, and if you have faith, you will receive it." (Matthew 21:22)

"God created everything through him, and nothing was created except through him." (John 1:3)

"Publish his glorious deeds among the nations. Tell everyone about the amazing things he does." (1 Chronicles 16:24)

"Enter his gates with thanksgiving and his courts with praise; give thanks to him and praise his name." (Psalm 100:4)

"Wait for the Lord; be strong and take heart and wait for the Lord." (Psalm 27:14)

ABOUT THE AUTHOR

As the wife of a small business owner and the mother of two, Susan Lee has discovered that it's never too late to grasp God's plans as our own and experience His best. She hopes that through her writing she can help others to discover God's unique plan for their lives and to Live Large For God! Connect with Susan Lee at **http://r50books.com/gloa**

While this is the end of the book, I hope you will stay in touch! If you enjoyed **God's Law of Attraction: The Believer's Guide to Success and Fulfillment,** please take the time to give me a review. Very few people take the time, so it is a really big deal if you do. I very much appreciate it. To leave a review, please visit my Author page at
amazon.com/author/susanleebooks

Please connect with me at **http://r50books.com/gloa**, or email me at **crew@r50books.com**

Recommended Reading:

Experience God's Law of Attraction Through Bible Verses and Spiritual Affirmations, By Susan Lee Available on Amazon.com

Developing Patience and Perseverance in an Impatient World, by Susan Lee Available on Amazon.com

Devotionals Reflecting on God's Power: What the Bible Teaches Us About Praise, Forgiveness, and More, by Susan Lee Available on Amazon.com

FREE BONUS!

Don't Forget to download your free bonus!

God's Law of Attraction Worksheets which will help you determine your goals, create positive affirmations, and combat negative beliefs.

Treasury of God's Promises is a collection of Bible verses that will help you focus on God's positive message.

Quotable Quotes is a selection of affirming quotes that will help you to keep God's powerful word in your heart.

In addition, you will be registered to receive new bonuses and gifts as they are added. To get all three gifts, just visit **R50Books.com/gloabonusreg**.

38438634R00048

Made in the USA
San Bernardino, CA
06 September 2016